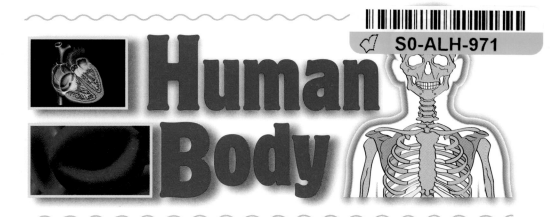

Human Body

BY MARC GAVE

Table of Contents

CHAPTER 1

Meet Your Body

You look very different now than you did at birth. Your body has changed a lot over the years. And it will continue to change throughout your life. How does your body grow? How does it carry out all the jobs it needs to do to keep you alive? How does it take care of itself? How does it let you know when things are right and when things are wrong?

You'll find some of the answers to these questions in this book. Once you get to know your body better, you'll probably be amazed at what a fantastic "machine" it is.

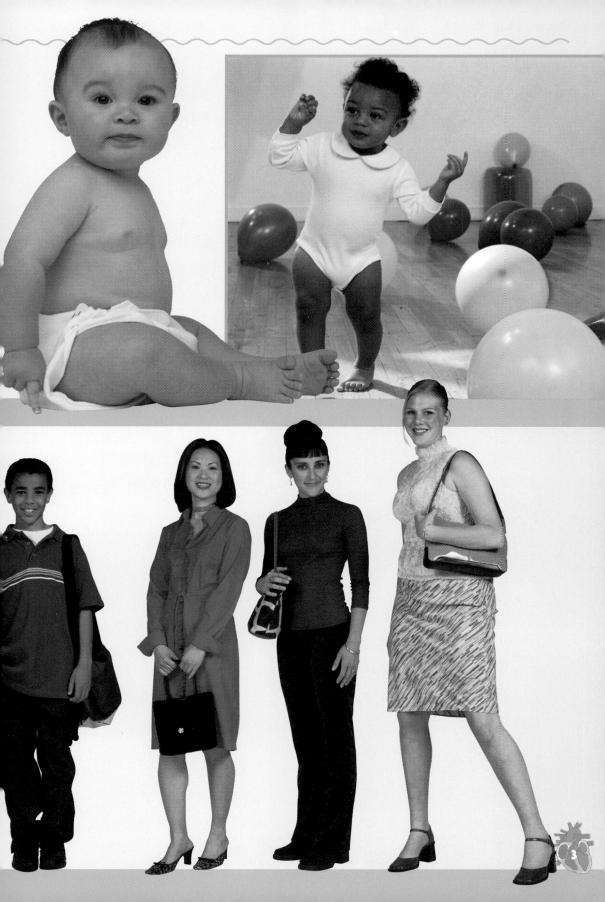

CHAPTER 2

What You See

You walk, run, eat, sleep, talk, laugh, sing, hop, jump, dive, swim, and study—to mention just a few common actions.

You also sneeze because something is annoying your nose. You sweat when you exercise, get warm, or are nervous. You cry when you are sad or happy. You hiccup if something is bothering your stomach.

Your body does all of these things and more. Along with looking at yourself in a mirror, these actions are the way you experience your body day in and day out.

- You sneeze at a speed of 75–100 miles an hour. That's as fast as some hurricanes travel or a pitcher sends a fastball toward home plate.

- You cough at a speed of about 300 miles an hour.

- Your hands and feet sweat more than any other parts of your body.

- You have about 100,000 hairs on your head. You lose between 50 and 100 a day, but they grow back. If you never got a haircut, your hair would grow about 25 feet long!

- Fingernails grow about an inch in eight months. Toenails take about two years to grow that much.

- You produce about a quart of saliva each day.

CHAPTER 3

Just One Cell

a model of a DNA molecule →

Great things start small, and you're no different. You began life as a single **cell**, a tiny piece of **matter** much too small to be seen without a microscope. Today your body contains billions of cells. Inside a cell are still smaller parts, each one with its own work to do.

Inside each cell is all the information that makes you who you are and keeps you alive. How can all that information fit inside a single cell? It's written in a special code called **DNA**. DNA is found in cell parts called **chromosomes** (KROH-muh-somz). These

a typical cell ↓

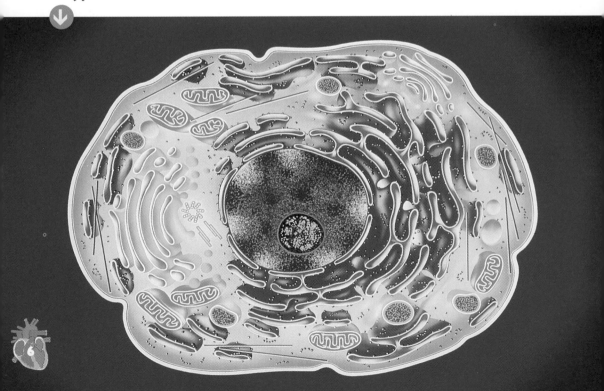

6

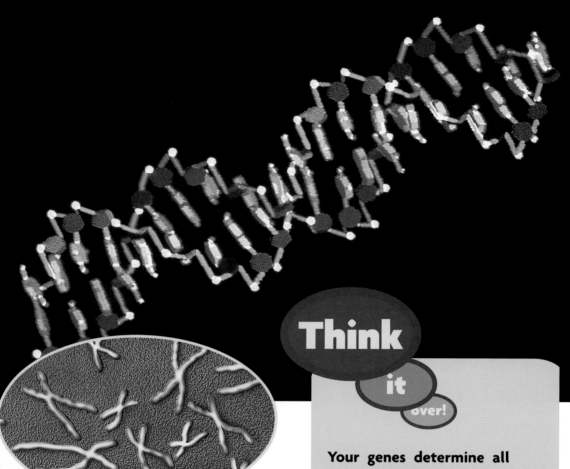

chromosomes

chromosomes contain **genes**. Genes are pieces of DNA that determine some aspect of the way you look or act.

Think it over!

Your genes determine all sorts of things about you—how tall you'll be, what color your skin, hair, and eyes are, what kind of mental and athletic skills you have.

Does that mean that there's nothing you can do to change your body? You can't really change the very basics. But eating well, sleeping, exercising, laughing, and avoiding harm can make a difference.

CHAPTER 4

Command Central

If there's one part of your body you couldn't do without, it's your brain. Your brain is the control center of the body. The functions of the brain are similar to those of the central processing unit of a computer. The brain sends and receives messages from all the other parts of your body through pathways that contain **nerve cells**.

Your brain contains about 35 billion nerve cells. When you are fully grown, it will weigh about three pounds. It's amazing that a relatively small part of your body has such a big job to do!

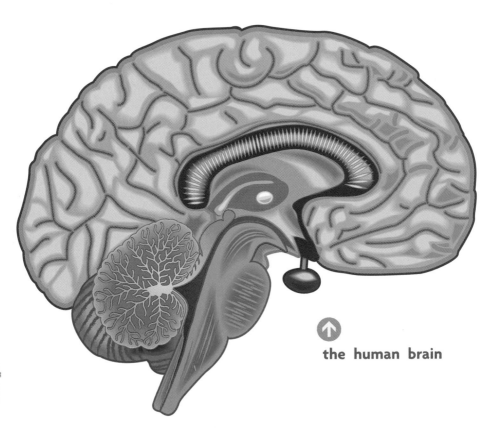

⬆ the human brain

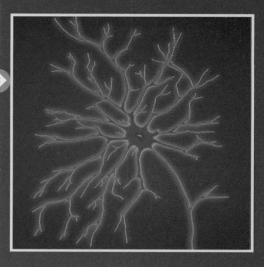

nerve cell →

The brain consists of three main parts. One part is the **brain stem**, which controls the activities of your heart, lungs, and other organs that keep you alive. It connects the brain to the **spinal cord**, which runs down the center of the back, and is surrounded by the bones of your spine. The other two parts of the brain are the **cerebrum** (suh-REE-bruhm) and the **cerebellum** (sair-uh-BEHL-uhm). Each is divided into two halves, which are linked by a thick band of nerves. The cerebrum is the largest part of the brain. It controls such things as moving, thinking, feeling, and memory. The cerebellum controls muscles and balance.

YOU'VE GOT SOME NERVES!

Some of your nerve cells are very long. One nerve cell runs from the bottom of your spine to your knee. But a nerve cell can be thinner than a single hair on your head. What kind of messages do nerve cells carry to and from the brain? Electrical ones. Yes, you really do run on electricity.

It's a **FACT!**

Is gray matter really gray? Yes. In the brain, densely packed nerve cell bodies that appear gray surround a smaller amount of white nerve fibers. The surface of this gray matter is quite wrinkled.

9

CHAPTER 5

Making Sense of It All

Your eyes, ears, nose, tongue, and skin are the parts of your body that allow you to sense the world around you. That's why sight, hearing, smell, taste, and touch are called the five senses.

Your ears pick up sound waves from the air and turn them into electrical messages to your brain. Your brain can store sound memories, too. You recognize a familiar voice or piece of music.

Your nose is the main place air enters your body. Cells there pick up smells from the air. In addition to allowing you to remember pleasant odors, storing smells helps you stay safe. You can "smell danger" in smoke and harmful chemicals.

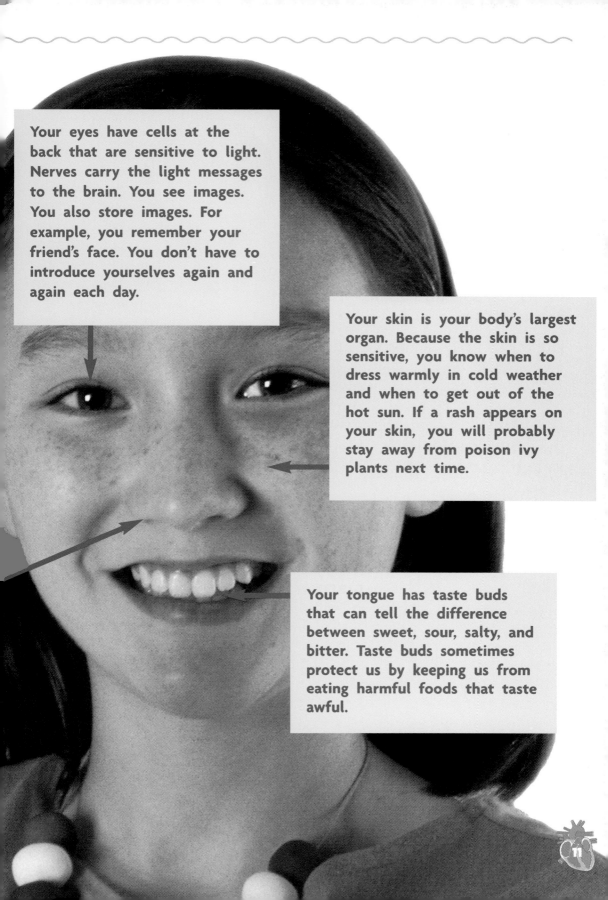

Your eyes have cells at the back that are sensitive to light. Nerves carry the light messages to the brain. You see images. You also store images. For example, you remember your friend's face. You don't have to introduce yourselves again and again each day.

Your skin is your body's largest organ. Because the skin is so sensitive, you know when to dress warmly in cold weather and when to get out of the hot sun. If a rash appears on your skin, you will probably stay away from poison ivy plants next time.

Your tongue has taste buds that can tell the difference between sweet, sour, salty, and bitter. Taste buds sometimes protect us by keeping us from eating harmful foods that taste awful.

CHAPTER 6

It's a Holdup

It's a FACT!

What allows you to stand up without collapsing and to perform a lot of physical activities? What protects your brain, heart, and lungs from injury? It's your bones, or skeleton. The skeleton gives support and shape to your body. It protects some of your organs. It allows you to move. And the bones of the skeleton contain minerals and are the places where blood cells are made.

Because bones are hard on the outside but hollow, they are strong and lightweight. The hollows are filled with soft, fatty **marrow,** which makes blood cells.

The longest bones in your body are your femurs, or thighbones. They are about one quarter of your total height. The smallest bones are in your ear. They are shaped like the stirrups used in horseback riding. These bones are only one eighth of an inch long!

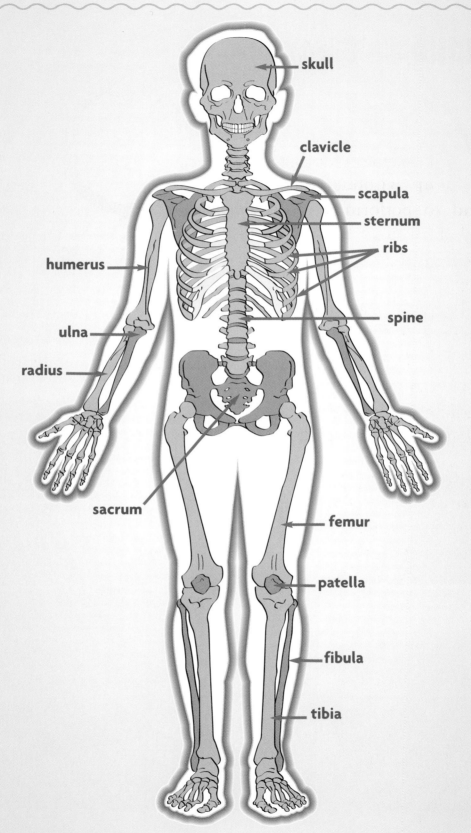

skull

clavicle

scapula

sternum

ribs

humerus

spine

ulna

radius

sacrum

femur

patella

fibula

tibia

CHAPTER 7

Make an Effort

Your skeleton doesn't work all by itself. It needs something to help move it. That's where your muscles come in.

If you've ever volunteered for anything, you know that you do it because you want to. Sometimes, it's the same with your body. You decide to bend over to pick up a pencil. You decide to shoot hoops. You decide to eat a juicy apple. These muscle movements are voluntary— you decide to make them.

Some muscles, such as your heart, move without your thinking about it. They are involuntary muscles.

Muscles are connected to the brain by nerves. The nerves carry electrical messages to the muscles that control when and how much the muscles should contract, or become shorter. As the muscles contract, they move the bones.

When you exercise, you make your muscles stronger. There are special exercises that are good for strengthening a certain muscle or a group of muscles.

FLEXING YOUR MUSCLES

Sit-ups strengthen your stomach and leg muscles. Push-ups develop your arms. Bending and stretching make your back more flexible. Some activities, such as swimming, cycling, and running are good for your breathing, too. Your body gets more air when you do them.

CHAPTER 8

Breathe Deeply

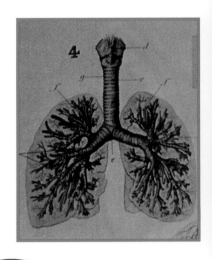

Getting enough oxygen from the air is something everybody has to do. Fortunately, you don't have to remind yourself to breathe. Like your heart beating, breathing is an involuntary action.

Why do you need oxygen? All the functions of life need energy. You get energy from the food you eat. But you need oxygen to burn up the food so it releases the energy it contains. When you breathe in, air goes to your lungs. Muscles near the lungs contract. This causes the lungs to fill with air. When the muscles relax, the air is pushed out.

It's a FACT!

At rest, you take about 12 breaths a minute. Without any other activity, that's 17,280 breaths in 24 hours!

Breathing may get two or three times faster when you run or are excited. If you keep breathing fast for a long time, you feel "out of breath."

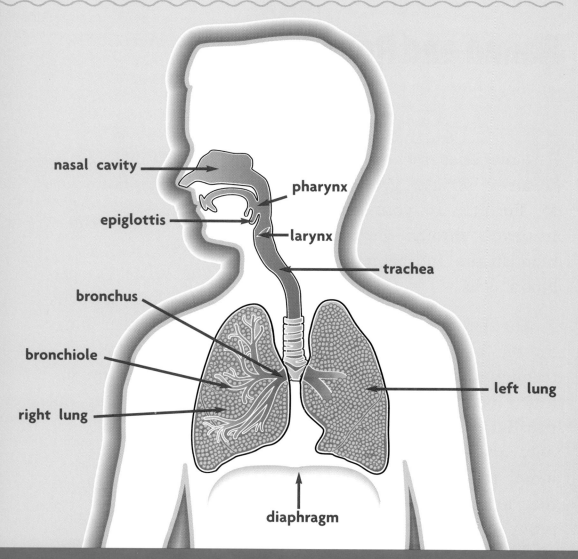

nasal cavity

pharynx

epiglottis

larynx

trachea

bronchus

bronchiole

right lung

left lung

diaphragm

THE AIR YOU BREATHE

Air is made of gases you can't see. About 78 percent of air is nitrogen. About 21 percent is oxygen. The rest is argon, carbon dioxide, hydrogen, neon, helium, and other gases. Our air has just the right amount of oxygen for living creatures to breathe.

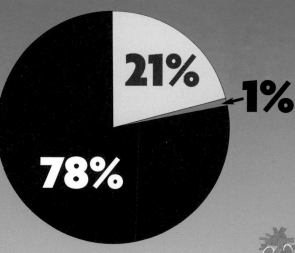

21%

1%

78%

CHAPTER 9

Round and Round

How does the oxygen you breathe get to all the cells of your body? It travels through the bloodstream in the red blood cells.

The red blood cells pick up the oxygen in the lungs through the thin walls of tiny blood vessels called **capillaries.** Capillaries are only one cell thick. The blood then travels back to the heart, where it is pumped into **arteries**. The arteries carry the oxygen-containing red blood cells to all parts of the body. The arteries get smaller and smaller as they get farther away from the heart. The oxygen is released as the arteries narrow into capillaries throughout your body.

As your cells use the fuel they need, they produce the waste gas carbon dioxide. This waste is carried back to your lungs in the red blood cells as the blood travels through the **veins**. You breathe out this waste.

How does the blood flow through your body? Your heart, which is a large muscle, keeps pumping it over and over.

The blood vessels carrying oxygen-rich blood to all the parts of the body are shown in red. These vessels are called arteries.

The blood vessels carrying oxygen-poor blood back to the heart and lungs are shown in blue. These vessels are called veins.

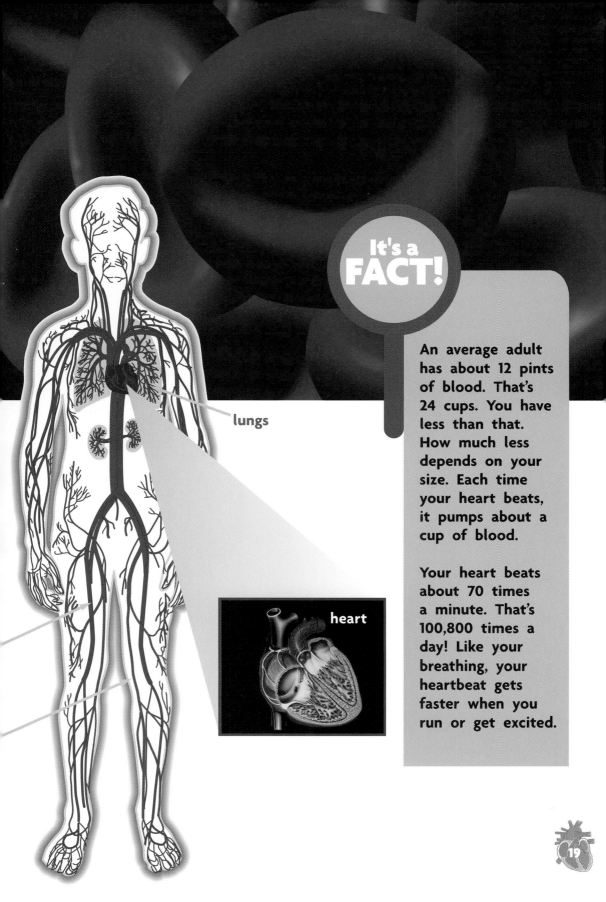

lungs

heart

An average adult has about 12 pints of blood. That's 24 cups. You have less than that. How much less depends on your size. Each time your heart beats, it pumps about a cup of blood.

Your heart beats about 70 times a minute. That's 100,800 times a day! Like your breathing, your heartbeat gets faster when you run or get excited.

CHAPTER 10

Are You Handy?

Y ou use your hands to do many things every day. So many, that it's not until you hurt your hand and cannot use it for a while that you realize just how important it is.

You can play ball and a musical instrument, wash yourself and the family car, write and type, get dressed and tie your shoes, draw and paint, build a birdhouse, pet your dog. That's just a small sample of the activities you do with your hands. You use your hand muscles differently for each action.

Some people are good at doing things that require strength in their hands. Others are better at doing things that require small, skillful movements. Finding out what your hands are good at can lead to hobbies you enjoy. It can also possibly guide you to the kind of work you will do when you grow up.

It's a FACT!

In 1995, students made a painting of Elvis Presley that covered more than 75,000 square feet. That's the area of about 25 large houses. It certainly took a lot of hands to accomplish!

20

CHAPTER 11

Fuel Up

You may have heard the expression "You are what you eat." In a way, it is true because food provides the energy and chemical substances that your body needs. One of these substances is **protein**, which is found mainly in meat, dairy products, nuts, and dried beans. Your body also needs **carbohydrates**, which are found in vegetables, fruits, and grains. Your body needs some animal or vegetable fat, too.

You also need to drink throughout the day in order to keep your body healthy. Drinking enough water is vital in hot weather or when doing hard work or exercise that makes you sweat a lot.

1 How does your body get what it needs from the food you eat? When you eat, you taste your food with your tongue, wet it with saliva, chew it with your teeth, and swallow it.

2 Food travels down your esophagus to your stomach.

3 In your stomach, food combines with **enzymes** and forms a smooth paste.

4 In the small intestine, the food is mixed with more enzymes and broken down, or digested, into chemical substances that your body can use. These substances pass through the wall of the small intestine. Those materials that your body cannot use move down into the large intestine.

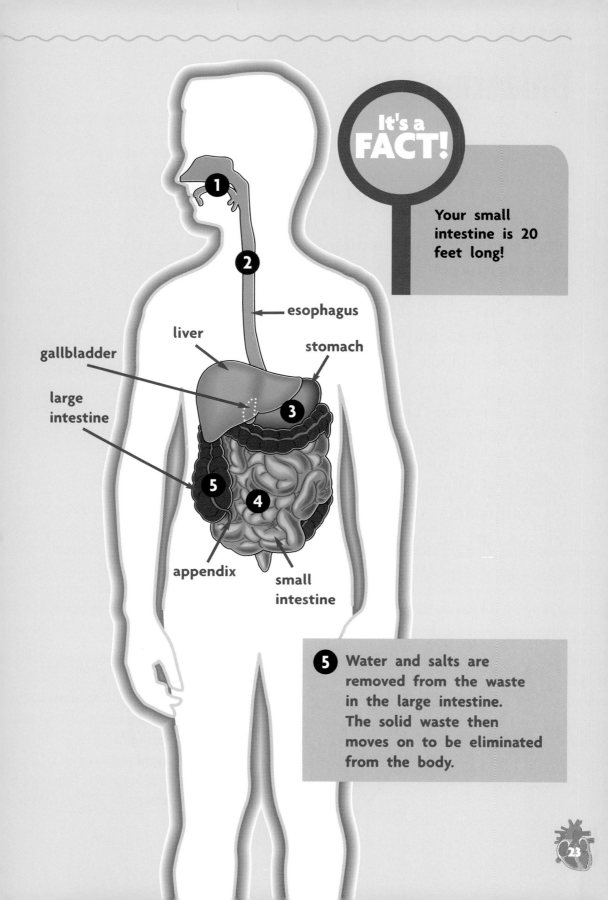

It's a
FACT!

Your small intestine is 20 feet long!

esophagus

liver

gallbladder

stomach

large intestine

appendix

small intestine

5 Water and salts are removed from the waste in the large intestine. The solid waste then moves on to be eliminated from the body.

CHAPTER 12

Balancing Acts

You have just learned how you digest your food. But several other organs play important roles in the process.

The liver—the largest and heaviest organ of the body—and the spleen keep your blood in good working order. The kidneys keep proper levels of salt in your body and also get rid of waste materials. The pancreas pours liquid into the small intestine to help it digest food. And **bile** from the gallbladder breaks up drops of fat that are in your food.

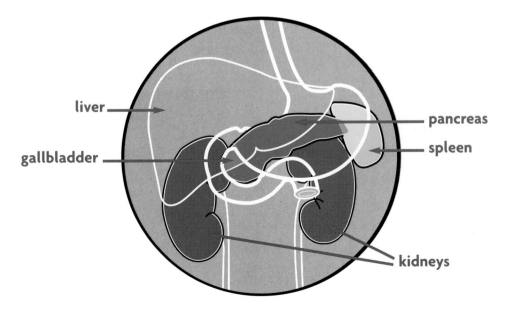

In your neck is the thyroid gland, which forms your "Adam's apple." The thyroid gland controls how fast your body makes energy from the food it takes in. The thyroid and other glands produce **hormones**, chemical substances that perform different tasks in different parts of your body. If glands aren't working properly, too little or too much of a hormone is made. In the case of the thyroid gland, the rate at which food is changed into energy can be too fast or too slow. Such a situation can affect the body's activities and even its emotions.

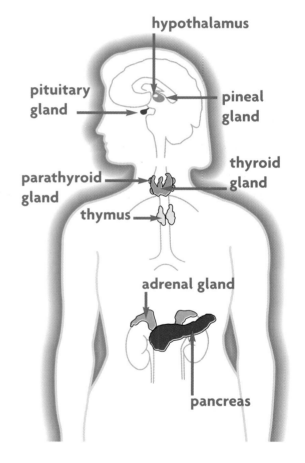

hypothalamus

pituitary gland

pineal gland

parathyroid gland

thyroid gland

thymus

adrenal gland

pancreas

CHAPTER 13

Invaders

It would be nice if we didn't have to worry about getting sick. But viruses, bacteria, and other tiny germs can enter our bodies and cause disease. How does the body protect us and keep us healthy?

The body has an **immune system**, whose job it is to defend the body against disease-causing germs.

The first line of defense against attack includes your skin, tears, and saliva. Sometimes, symptoms let you know that these defenses are under attack. Redness, heat, swelling, and pain indicate that infection has occurred and that your body is fighting the infection.

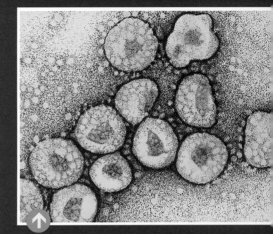

common cold

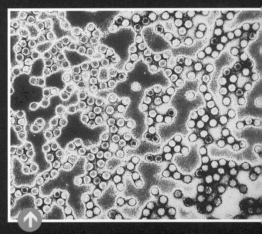

polio

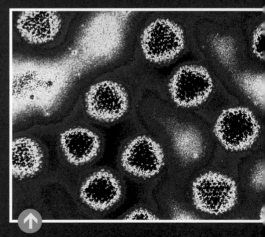

adenovirus

If the first line of defense fails, specific cells usually develop to fight a specific invader. This second line of defense works only after the invasion has occurred. Once your body has successfully fought off an invader, it can "remember" the invader and fight it off again if it returns. The cells usually attack only the invaders, not healthy parts of the body.

Sometimes, you can't produce your own defenses against infection. That's when you go to the doctor and get a shot. Some shots, such as the ones you get for measles, prevent you from getting a specific disease. Others, such as a shot of penicillin, help you fight off germs that have already made you sick.

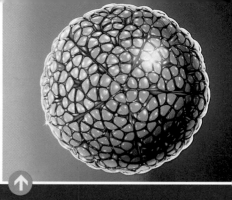
rotavirus

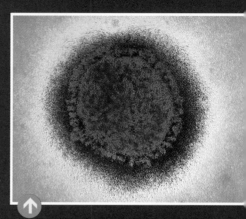
influenza virus

It's a
FACT!

Penicillin, one of many medicines that fight germs, was discovered by accident in 1928. While doing some experiments in his lab, Alexander Fleming noticed that mold had begun to grow on a sample of germs he was growing. The mold had killed some of the germs! The mold was *penicillium*. About ten years later, penicillin began to be used to kill germs in people.

27

Your Body for Life

You can help your body fight disease by making it as strong as possible. You need to eat a balanced diet and get enough sleep and exercise. You must follow good health habits—washing, brushing your teeth, and taking care of cuts and other places where germs can invade.

As you grow, your body's needs will change. You may go through a time of rapid growth or you may grow steadily over a longer period of time. Your body will also change in ways that prepare you for becoming a grown-up.

Just as it is important to do the right things for your body, it is important not to do the wrong things. Smoking, drinking alcohol, taking drugs, and putting yourself in dangerous situations can seriously harm you. You've got only one body, and you need to treat it right.

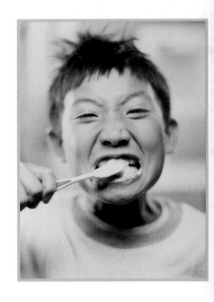

It seems amazing that the systems of your body work so well, individually and together, so much of the time. Learning as much as you can about how your body works will help you understand why you feel healthy or not so healthy. Listening to your body is one of the most basic, yet most difficult things to do. You can keep your body in top shape by knowing the healthful things to do and the unhealthful things to avoid. Start putting what you have learned into action.

Glossary

arteries	large blood vessels that carry oxygen-rich blood from the heart to all parts of the body
bile	fluid made by the liver and stored in the gallbladder that breaks down fat in the body
brain stem	part of the brain that controls the activity of your heart, lungs, and other parts of your body that keep you alive
capillaries	the smallest blood vessels in your body
carbohydrates	chemical compounds found in vegetables, fruits, and grains
cell	the smallest unit of living *matter*
cerebellum	part of the brain that controls muscles and balance
cerebrum	part of the brain that controls moving, thinking, feeling, and memory
chromosomes	tiny parts of cells that contain the *genes*
DNA	chemical compound that makes up *genes*
enzymes	*proteins* made by cells that help different parts of the body do their work
genes	parts of *chromosomes* that control one or more traits that one living thing passes along to the next generation
hormones	chemical substances produced by glands of the body and carried in the blood to control growth and energy
immune system	group of body parts that fights disease
marrow	the soft filling of bones, in which red *cells* and many white *cells* are made
matter	anything that has mass (weight) and takes up space
nerve cells	*cells* in the brain, *spinal cord*, and nerves that send electric messages controlling how the body works
protein	any of numerous chemical compounds found in meat, dairy products, nuts, and dried beans
spinal cord	the mass of nerve tissue that runs along the backbone and carries messages to and from the brain
veins	large blood vessels that carry oxygen-poor blood back to the heart and lungs from the rest of the body

Index